For Arden Myrin and Jonathan Beal, my funny people
—A.G.

For Claire and Chloe, with love and laughter
—J.T.

To Rose and Hazel, my own funny ladies
—B.B.

The illustrations in this book were rendered in radiant watercolor ink and Photoshop.

Cataloging-in-Publication Data has been applied for and may be obtained from the Library of Congress.

ISBN 978-1-4197-4992-6

Text © 2024 Amy Guglielmo and Jacqueline Tourville
Illustrations © 2024 Brigette Barrager
Book design by Heather Kelly

Printed and bound in China
10 9 8 7 6 5 4 3 2 1

Abrams Books for Young Readers are available at special discounts when purchased in quantity for premiums
and promotions as well as fundraising or educational use. Special editions can also be created to specification.
For details, contact specialsales@abramsbooks.com or the address below.

ABRAMS The Art of Books
195 Broadway, New York, NY 10007
abramsbooks.com

Lucy!

How Lucille Ball Did It All

by AMY GUGLIELMO
and JACQUELINE TOURVILLE

illustrated by
BRIGETTE BARRAGER

Abrams Books for Young Readers

New York

Back in a time when children were told to be proper, calm, and quiet, a girl named Lucy hopped up onto the counter of Mr. Newman's general store, puffed out her cheeks, and let out a great, big . . .

"Riiibbit!"

Lucy's mother giggled. Mr. Newman hooted. Chuckling customers tossed pennies and candies.

And Lucy grinned—making people laugh made her heart burst with happiness.

But in 1914, girls weren't allowed to be loud, and they weren't supposed to be funny.

Still, brave, sassy, silly Lucy couldn't help herself. She just loved the sound of laughter.

And she loved the joy she felt while laughing, too—like when her father tossed her high in the air, making her shriek with glee.

But when Lucy was very young, her father died. She missed his laugh—a roar like a lion's—every day.

Not long after that, Lucy's mother needed to move away to look for work. Lucy and her brother had to go stay with dour relatives, who frowned at Lucy's antics and ordered her to stop goofing around.

Whenever she could, Lucy played alone in the attic with her clothespin dolls. She told them jokes and made funny faces. She could almost hear her dolls' titters and tee-hees—but it wasn't the same as real laughter.

So when Lucy's mother returned, and her kind grandparents announced that they wanted their whole family to come live with them, Lucy let out a whoop and quickly packed her bags!

Jamestown had a snazzy theater and a swell amusement park. All summer long, people strolled the boardwalk, calliope music chimed, and the Ferris wheel spun.

Lucy's family was poor, so it was a treat when her grandpa took her to see a vaudeville show. The actors danced, sang songs, and performed skits that put the audience in stitches.

Mesmerized by the crowd's thunderous reaction, Lucy wanted to be the person on stage who delighted people with laughter. Laughter brought families together. It made people forget their troubles. It was pure love.

Back at home, she made up her own shows, imagining herself on stage. Lucy and her brother wrote songs and performed zany scenes.

They made Grandpa guffaw, Grandma cheer, Mama chortle and clap. Taking a bow, Lucy beamed. Putting smiles on people's faces was the best feeling!

A few years later, Lucy landed a part in the school comedy. Finally, she would be on a *real* stage making people laugh!

Lucy worked tirelessly preparing for her big debut. She practiced lines, sewed costumes, and even dragged her mother's couch to school to serve as a prop.

On opening night, Lucy came alive under the lights. When the audience roared, Lucy realized she had a genuine talent for making people happy.

As she got older, she became eager to improve her skills, spread joy, and become a real star. Lucy begged her mother to send her to an acting school in New York City.

Lucy's mother scrimped and saved until, at long last, she said yes.
But New York City was not what Lucy had imagined. It was gray and
gritty, and the busy people on the streets scowled.

And acting school was no laughing matter!

Lucy's drama teacher told her that in order to be a great actress, she must be serious, not silly. He gave her pages and pages of scripts to memorize. All the lines were somber and glum.

When Lucy stood center stage, she didn't feel bold or brave. For the first time in her life, she felt nervous and shy. For the first time, she didn't feel like laughing. She forgot her lines and could barely speak above a whisper.

Lucy's teacher mailed her mother a stern note:

"Lucy's wasting her time and ours!"

Still, stubborn Lucy stuck it out. Even when, at audition after audition, she heard . . .

"You can't dance!"
"You can't sing!"
"You can't act!"

. . . Lucy didn't give up—and then finally, she earned a role as a Broadway chorus girl. And after that, she got her lucky break: a tiny part in a Hollywood movie!

Her first day on the studio lot, Lucy was eager to perform—but she was directed to stand silently in the background with a group of other "Goldwyn girls" picked to fill out the scene. Once again, Lucy wouldn't get to be her silly, sassy self.

Until clever Lucy had an idea: She'd show them what made her special.

When the movie's star came over to say hello, Lucy knew just how to make him chuckle.

"She's a riot!" he declared.

And when the director needed an actor to take a pie to the face, Lucy was the first to volunteer.

"Get that girl's name," the director demanded. "That's the one who'll make it."

From there, Lucy began to land more films, but they were still only bit parts—small roles that didn't show her talent. Being a funny lady in Hollywood wasn't easy.

But Lucy persisted. She took more acting lessons and studied with comedian Buster Keaton to hone her slapstick skills. And when movies changed to Technicolor . . .

Lucy colored her hair bright red, so no one could forget her.

Her grit and moxie paid off: Over the next ten years, she appeared in more than sixty movies. But she kept feeling like her on-screen persona was wooden and flat, because she wasn't allowed to play her roles as she wanted.

Lucy wondered if she would ever find a place to sparkle and be herself. Always eager to explore new ways to perform, she started working in radio.

One day, Lucy accepted a role in a radio comedy show. She played a rebellious and funny housewife, at a time when housewives were supposed to be pretty, proper, and polite.

She recorded the show in front of a live audience, which allowed her to get the enthusiastic reaction she yearned for. *My Favorite Husband* was a hit!

In fact, the show was so successful, CBS asked her to bring it to television. This new form of entertainment seemed risky, but now Lucy had an opportunity to make her mark—as the star of her own show.

Always bold and ever determined, Lucy convinced the network to let her real husband, Desi, play her husband in the show; she knew their laughter would be contagious.

She also requested a live studio audience, so she could hear their genuine laughter.

And she insisted that she be a producer—the first woman in showbiz history to run a television studio!

I Love Lucy debuted on October 15, 1951. The show was an immediate sensation! Every Monday at nine o'clock, all of America stopped to laugh at Lucy's wacky antics.

At last, she had landed the perfect role.

They finally let Lucy be *Lucy!*

But best of all was the laughter. Taping each show before her audience, Lucy got to hear the giggles, snorts, hoots, and lionlike roars she'd been chasing all her life. She had taken television by storm, and she had made it her own.

Lucy loved to make them laugh.

And many, many years later . . .

AUTHORS' NOTE

*"I'm not talented. I can't sing and I can't dance.
I just have an obsession to make people laugh.
I don't know why, but I love hearing people laugh."*

—Lucille Ball

More than a century ago, before the days of movie theaters, traveling vaudeville acts delighted and amused audiences with live comedy sketches and song-and-dance routines. It was mostly male actors who had all the funny lines, but that didn't stop a young girl named Lucille Ball—Lucy—from dreaming that someday, she would be the one on stage getting all the laughs and applause.

Born August 6, 1911, Lucy was only fourteen years old when she moved to New York City to attend the John Murray Anderson-Robert Milton School of Theater and Dance. Future movie star Bette Davis was one of Lucy's classmates! Bette wowed the school's acting teachers with her talent for drama. Lucy was not so lucky. Still, despite being told at audition after audition that she had no talent, determined Lucy channeled her grit and kept chasing her dreams.

Lucy finally got her big break—a trip to Hollywood and a contract with MGM studios. She was cast as one of the twelve Goldwyn Girls in the movie *Roman Scandals*, directed by Frank Tuttle and choreographed by Busby Berkeley. From there, she found plenty of work as an actress in Hollywood, but she always ended up in the "B" movies: the nickname for movies that ran before the main features with the big stars. Lucy made so many of these movies that she was called the "Queen of the Bs." It was on the set of one of these "B" films—*Dance, Girl, Dance*—that Lucille Ball met and fell in love with one her costars, Cuban bandleader Desi Arnaz. They were married in 1940. Sadly, their marriage ended in divorce in 1960.

And about that red hair . . . She was a natural brunette! Lucy changed her hair color to its signature flaming red shade in 1943 for a movie part. It was a hit, and Lucy kept her hair red for the rest of her life.

In the late 1940s, Lucy starred on the CBS radio show *My Favorite Husband*. Its success helped the determined Lucy finally get what she'd always wanted. In 1951, *I Love Lucy*, the first TV show starring a female comedian, took to the television airwaves and became an instant sensation. Lucy's antics kept her live studio audience roaring—the show holds the record for receiving the longest laugh in television history. It was so long—67 seconds—that it had to be cut down for the final airing! And Lucy's real mom was present at every filming of the show. She can sometimes be heard saying "Uh-oh!" in the audience.

I Love Lucy broke barriers in other ways. Desi was the first Latino actor to star in an American TV show. *I Love Lucy* was also the first series to show a visibly pregnant woman on television, when Lucy was pregnant in real life with her son, Desi Jr.

The show has been translated into dozens of languages and still airs in reruns around the globe today. It's estimated that over forty million people watch *I Love Lucy* EVERY SINGLE YEAR!

In 1962, Lucy became the first woman to run a major television studio. Desilu Productions not only made *I Love Lucy*, but also went on to produce *Star Trek*, *Mission: Impossible*, and many other famous shows.

Lucille Ball received numerous awards throughout her lifetime, including four Emmys, the Golden Globe Cecil B. DeMille Award, the Lifetime Achievement Award from the Kennedy Center Honors, two stars on the Hollywood Walk of Fame, and the Governors Award from the Academy of Television Arts & Sciences. The National Comedy Center and the Lucille Ball Desi Arnaz Museum are both located in Lucy's hometown, Jamestown, New York.

We love Lucy for so many reasons:

* Because she was loud and silly at a time when girls were expected to be quiet and well-behaved.

* Because she had the pluck to dream big dreams even when times were tough.

* Because she had the determination and grit to break down barriers for women in Hollywood.

* Because she embraced what made her special and stayed true to herself, no matter what.

* Because at a time when women were told they couldn't be funny, Lucy got the last laugh.

And, of course . . .

* Because no one can make us laugh like Lucy.

"The more things you do, the more you can do."

—*Lucille Ball*

BIBLIOGRAPHY

Ball, Lucille. *Love, Lucy*. New York: Putnam, 1996.

Harris, Warren G. *Lucy and Desi: The Legendary Love Story of Television's Most Famous Couple*. New York: Simon & Schuster, 1991.

Kanfer, Stefan. *Ball of Fire: The Tumultuous Life and Comic Art of Lucille Ball*. New York: Alfred A. Knopf, 2003.

Sanders, Coyne Steven, and Tom Gilbert. *Desilu: The Story of Lucille Ball and Desi Arnaz*. New York: Dey Street Books, 2011.